"This beautiful translation introduces to an English reading audience Mohammed Ghassani's captivating poetry. It is representative of new, young, confident, patriotic, hopeful, and vibrant voices currently emerging out of a long tradition of Kiswahili verse. This is a daring voice very much worth listening to."
—ABDILATIF ABDALLA, Kenyan political activist, author of *Sauti ya Dhiki* (Voice of Agony), and retired teacher of Kiswahili language and African literature at the University of Leipzig

"The journeys Mohammed Ghassani's poetry beautifully takes raise questions about home: Is it a place that only poetry can find? Is it a road map back home or is poetry itself the destination, our final home? In Meg Arenberg's translation is home to be found in many languages? And for the reader, do you now see you live in many homes? Come to Ghassani's poetry all packed and prepared, with your arms wide open ready to embrace your many selves. Home here is a train traveling faster than the speed of light to all destinations at the same time."
—MUKOMA WA NGUGI, cofounder of the Safal-Cornell Kiswahili Prize for African Literature and author of *Logotherapy*

I HAVE A HOME, THERE IS A WE

I HAVE A HOME, THERE IS A WE

Voice of a Stranger in a Strange Land

Mohammed Khelef Ghassani

Translated by Meg Arenberg

University of Nebraska Press
Lincoln

First published in Kiswahili as *N'na Kwetu: Sauti ya Mgeni Ugenini* © 2021, 2016 by Mohammed Khelef Ghassani
Translation © 2026 by Meg Arenberg

"Too Many," "The Butterfly Fish," and "I Am a Leaf" previously appeared in Sofia Amina, ed., *The Black Anthology, Language* (London: 1010 Press, 2021), 26–33.

The University of Nebraska Press is part of a land-grant institution with campuses and programs on the past, present, and future homelands of the Pawnee, Ponca, Otoe-Missouria, Omaha, Dakota, Lakota, Kaw, Cheyenne, and Arapaho Peoples, as well as those of the relocated Ho-Chunk, Sac and Fox, and Iowa Peoples.

♾

The African Poetry Book Series is operated by the African Poetry Book Fund (APBF). The founding director of the APBF is Kwame Dawes, Professor of Literary Arts at Brown University. Established in 2012 by Kwame Dawes at the University of Nebraska–Lincoln with initial support from late philanthropists Laura and Robert F. X. Sillerman, the APBF now operates in partnership with Brown University.

For customers in the EU with safety/GPSR concerns, contact: gpsr@mare-nostrum.co.uk
Mare Nostrum Group BV
Mauritskade 21D
1091 GC Amsterdam
The Netherlands

Library of Congress Control Number: 2025029934

Set in Garamond Premier Pro by L. Welch.
Designed by N. Putens.

CONTENTS

TRANSLATOR'S NOTE

When I was first asked by the board of the Safal-Cornell Kiswahili Prize for African Literature to translate this collection—the inaugural winner in the poetry category—now nearly a decade ago, I was not familiar with Mohammed Ghassani's work. In the intervening years his voice has become a familiar companion, and Ghassani himself a friend and brother to me. His consistent warmth, his generosity talking me through the personal and political contexts of these poems, and his patience relating various particularities of Kipemba—the dialect of Kiswahili specific to his home island of Pemba, to which he is so dedicated and in which he writes with such eloquence—have immeasurably improved the translations. We have been in frequent touch, meeting virtually and in person many times over the course of this project. Most importantly, we have read out loud together, bringing the poems alive and into dialogue across languages and continents, for ourselves and for others.

Even so, this is a book that has resisted completion. Some of the resistance has surely been due to my own meandering process as a translator, the time I have needed for sitting with the work, even after many revisions. Some perhaps has been due to the recalcitrance of English in accepting the steady rhythms, soft rhymes, and often proclamatory modes of Kiswahili prosody. Carrying these poems over, rendering them anew, has necessitated the dismantling and reconstruction of their form, and different poems have suggested different strategies. Slant rhymes and loose meter rose more naturally out of my translations of some poems than others. At the least, I have worked to preserve Ghassani's attentiveness to sound and the subtle power a repetitive pattern can accrue over the course of a poem. Where I felt I could, I have maintained verse length, approximate line length, and punctuation, and the order of the poems is unchanged from the original. In all cases, I have prioritized remaining true to the emotional force of Ghassani's voice, even where its chords may ring somewhat unfamiliar to an English reader's ear. To the extent that I have been successful in reproducing some flavor of his collection, it is the insistent beauty, playfulness, and passion of Ghassani's writing that have pushed me to stay the course. I am immensely grateful for his trust in my ability to do so, and for this opportunity to introduce his work to a wider community of readers.

I would also be remiss not to acknowledge my debt to the innumerable translators, writers, and lovers of Kiswahili literature who have supported me and this project in all manner of ways throughout its journey; they include, but are by no means limited to: Abdilatif Abdalla, Flavia Aiello, Ann Biersteker, Irene Brunotti, Annmarie Drury, Berenike Eichhorn, Karen Emmerich, Roberto Gaudioso, Lizi Geballe, Wangui wa Goro, Ida Hadjivayanis, Hajj Mohammed Hajj, Ali Hilal, Bill Johnston, Aurelie Journo, Nathalie Arnold Koenings, Kai Kresse, Patrick Malloy, M. Yunus Rafiq, Bhakti Shringarpure, and Clarissa Vierke. To each of you: asante sana. You have made this work possible.

MEG ARENBERG

It was a Wednesday. The date was September 1, 2010. The time around 10:00 p.m. The place was J. K. Nyerere International Airport in Dar es Salaam, the economic capital of the United Republic of Tanzania. I remember everything about that day. As I sat in the international departures lounge, I pulled out my cell phone and called a few people to say goodbye. Among them were my two mothers—the one who birthed me, Abeida bint Nassor, and the one who raised me, Salaa bint Said—my wife, Tauhida bint Mkwale, and my sister, Fatma bint Khelef.

These would be my last conversations on Tanzanian soil for a full year and a half. And that period would come to be, without question, the longest consecutive span I would live away from my home, Zanzibar. Our words weren't only of farewell but of mutual encouragement. The three of them, my two mothers and my wife, I had left under one roof in our home in Mwanyanya, on Zanzibar Island. And our youngest child at that time, Abdunaeem, had been born only two weeks previous. His picture was fixed in my mind as the feelings unleashed by leaving them behind washed over me. I remember my birth mother telling me, "Go, my son. Insha'Allah, nothing here will go wrong!" I remember my surrogate mother telling me, "God protect you, my child. We are in his hands!" My wife cried as she said a prayer, and my daughter, Ghanima, called out, "Papa, Papa!" She asked a question that she would come to ask every time I talked to her: "But when are you coming home?" Each and every time I answered, I would fall to the ground in tears.

These feelings have remained with me, even after my wife and our four children came to join me in Germany a year and a half later. Every day, every hour, every minute of this period I have lived in a state of internal anguish and self-doubt. I have chastised myself continuously for my decision to leave the life of a native in my homeland for the life of a foreigner in this foreign place. Feelings of loss have always been with me.

One night, in the dark and bitter cold, I woke in my tiny room and cried alone as I asked myself unanswerable questions:

Home, o home, our place how I remember you
In the dark, here in the dark, the tears come falling down
Why, o why, did I ever go away?

Loneliness, o loneliness, cloaks me like a shroud
It kills me this, it kills, and soon I will be buried
If only, if only, I were able to escape

But was I willing to continue living in personal suffering? I asked this of myself a few days later as a means of self-soothing, though the answer to this question continued to rend my heart rather than making it whole.

On the one hand, the question reminded me of the basic truth that the world we live in is a world of comings and goings. Since the prophet Noah was ordered to board his ark with his animals and to disembark onto this earth of our Creator God, the universe has been a terrain of departure and arrival. In times of peace and war, happiness and sorrow, in political harmony and social disorder, our world has been filled with immigrants and emigrants. Every day the sun rises, people leave one part of the world and make their way toward another.

With these few examples I gave myself heart. What to you is a place left behind is to another a destination. I am sure that within these seven years of living on foreign land, making this place my home and the home of my children, hundreds of foreigners have made our home, Zanzibar, their own and the home of their children. And so, at least on this side, I found myself settling into a kind of normalcy—a commonplace of the human condition, of history, of nature itself—the state of leaving and arriving.

But there was another side for me, an aspect that offered me no comfort at all. I had already been an emigrant and an immigrant—if it could be called that—within the land of my own country, Zanzibar. I use those words only because of the reality I faced—for better and for worse.

The story starts in 1996, a year and a half after my father died. I moved from the island of Pemba where I was born and raised, and moved to the island of Unguja for school. These are the two major islands that make up the Zanzibar archipelago, along with a number of smaller islands. I remember a short time before the MV Serengeti pulled up its anchor at Mkoani Port at the southern tip of Pemba, I pulled out a pen and paper and wrote this poem to say goodbye to my island:

MY KHADHIRA, HUSH NOW
Khadhira, this journey I embark on
Don't think I am uprooting, disappearing from your view
I do not go by choice but out of obligation
So accept, my love, accept; let me go now with your blessing
Then listen to me closely
This voyage will return
No matter what I find there, I won't turn my back on you

In truth, that move changed me. I became "mwanakutokomea," like a latch that cannot fasten. That is to say, since the day I left I have not returned to the life I lived growing up on Pemba island. Since that time, my returns have only been short visits. I have not yet kept my promise not to leave my "Khadhira" for whatever it was I would find abroad.

Even so, I have gained much from my emigration and immigration. In the fourteen years that I lived on Unguja Island I accomplished a great deal in my personal life—education, career, marriage, and family. It was during this time that I was hired by the tourism company Fisherman Tours and Travel Ltd. and by the State University of Zanzibar (SUZA) at the same time. It was also during that period that I joined the first independent newspaper *Dira Zanzibar* and became an occasional writer of criticism in various newspapers coming out of Dar es Salaam. I also joined forces with the director of news for the Civic United Front (CUF) as news desk editor. As such, I counted that first period of leaving and arriving as one of great fortune for myself and those who surrounded me. Alhamudullilah, it gave me the opportunity to lift myself up and improve my quality of life in an environment where thousands of young people my age hadn't had similar luck. In each of these instances, I didn't have time to sit back and ruminate on my journey because things were going my way.

But I came to know the painful truth of emigration and immigration within my own country when my rights as a citizen became entangled with my political persuasions. When I went to exercise my right to vote in 2000 (and in all the major and minor elections between 2000 and 2010), I was reminded by the election authorities that I was an "immigrant" and voting wasn't my right. The law in Zanzibar grants any Zanzibari of eighteen years of age with a resident card of identification the right to vote as long as he has been in the area where he votes for three years before registering. Even so, the final decision of who votes is not determined by these laws but by the arbitrary authority of the government officers, the "sheha" who have the reputation of being guardians of the administration in power. The result is that those with the right to vote are deprived of that right simply because they are not members of the ruling party, and those who should not have the right are granted it so long as they are believed to be aligned with those in power. I was on the side of the opposition. I wrote the poem "Kipande cha Kura" ("Ballot") to approximate the incident that happened to me alongside similar incidents that happened to others in my position:

> I pronounced my name, "So-in-so bin so-in-so."
> And the sheha jumped. "What house is it you stay in?"
> In fact, this sheha—he was also my neighbor
> I told him "Matuleni, and I'm sure you know the way"
>
> So the sheha rose to his feet, looked inside his book
> Among the listed names, he said, he didn't find me

"I don't know this man," he announced to the gathered crowd
All those years as neighbors, in an instant he denied me

Another truth about comings and leavings that gives me no comfort is that people have come to assume only certain motivations for an immigrant to move from a country of the so-called Third World—Africa, Arabia, Asia and South America—to a country we are told is in the First World. These are considered distinct from immigration in the other direction, that is, from the nations of the First World to the Third World.

When an immigrant comes from the First World he is understood to be an investor, a specialist, or a tourist. The general assumption for an immigrant coming from the Third World is that he has been lured by the luxuries of life in the First World, away from the troubles and suffering of the place he's left behind. The general picture is that he is poor, escaping to a place of riches, a martyr to heroic governments, running for his life, or a stateless person seeking cover. In his soul, he is expected to accept these interpretations of his reasoning and to interpret his own migration in this way. That's how it is in the minds of many, not just among those who welcome him in the foreign land but those he leaves behind in his own.

And to this you can add another bitter truth: Many immigrants who come to First World nations, or who attempt to, come from Arab and North African countries where civil war has taken over, and so, as they say, *pumu imepata mkohozi*, the cough has found its throat. If that weren't enough, there is also the truth that many of the explosions understood as acts of terrorism in the First World—from America, France, and Belgium to England and Spain— are said to be done either by immigrants or the children of immigrants. This has been sufficient to stereotype all immigrants as dangerous people, coming from dangerous places and spreading peril, and as a result harsh conservative policies are popping up and gaining traction all over the First World to resist travelers and immigrants!

My mind has refused these interpretations of the Third World immigrant on First World soil. I can't deny the reality in many Third World countries, including my own. Many are poor in terms of income and have weak economies. I won't refute either the claim that many are ruled by ignorant governments that deny their citizens rights and freedoms that would allow them to develop themselves and their communities. But it is not the case that every immigrant from those countries who is now in the First World is there because he is a victim of these plights. Rather, there are many who come for reasons aside from those, including a desire to learn, to see the world, and even to invest. It doesn't mean that they don't have a home to go back to, but rather that they have made the decision to leave their homes and experience the world!

Another extremely important matter that nags at my soul in this life abroad is how to raise my children. They are the ones I take to be victims of a decision they had no part in making. They are not the ones who decided to live far from the soil that birthed them and where their umbilical cords are buried. I am the one who tore them from our home when they were too young to know what place to call theirs and where to make their lives. Now that they are getting older, I am witnessing what I have taken from their lives and that which I have attempted to give them with this decision of mine. I have deprived them of their native tongue—the fullness and eloquence of Kiswahili—and have given them another they didn't cut their teeth on. I have denied them proud citizenship in a place that is ours collectively and have given them the confusion of a different homeplace, one that, to be sure, is foreign to them, even though it is their home. This pledge to choose for them at a time when they had no choice but to follow my desires causes me to question deeply this thing that I have done. This is why, a year after they joined me here in this foreign place, I wrote the poem "Wanangu Nisameheni" ("My Children, Forgive Me"):

> Please don't indict me, my children, understand me
> Please don't strike me, I'm already at my grave
> Please don't deride me or think ill of my name
> As for the good for which I'm still searching
> My children, it will be yours
> And if I fail to provide it, my children, forgive me

And so, this collection *N'na Kwetu* is a representation of the war I have fought within myself. It is the outcome of the weeping in the middle of the night of a migrant who still interrogates his decision to leave his home and immigrate to a foreign place. It is the confession of a father who was born and raised in a culture he would like to see taken up by the next generation, but who watches his children growing and becoming increasingly accustomed to a culture that he doesn't understand and that isn't his own. It is the story of a migrant who lives in two worlds, who tries to knit them together and to knit himself to them, and in doing so to connect his children to this chain of cultures. It is the story of an immigrant who believed he could draw these disparate parts together and live with all of them without their frustrating and harming one another, but who finds himself unfulfilled.

Even so, one important thing to say here is that I have incomparable and profound gratitude to the nation of Germany for receiving me seven years ago and welcoming my family a year and a half later, and for giving all of us the opportunity to better ourselves and to grow our skills and gifts. In this short time, I have already learned so much that I could not have learned in all the years I lived at home. Germany has given me the opportunity to fulfill many goals and with the great faith of my hosts, from my workplace where I was employed to the official institutions of the country, to an extent that perhaps even the authorities in my own country wouldn't believe, either because of my political stance or because of not knowing my capacities in those areas or even because of not having a system within which my skills could be recognized and given a chance.

If there is anything I regret in coming to live here abroad, it is not missing out on opportunities or faith but rather in leaving my country when it needed me and in recognizing that, regardless of what it has or doesn't have, it is mine. They say, "Only Mama is Mama." No one else can compare, no matter how sweet. I have the fortune of two mothers, the one who birthed me and the one who raised me, and both have remained mothers to me.

The decision to move with all my earthly possessions from the land where my placenta was buried and to settle far from it has given me the experience of living in different worlds. But I still have memories of my home in the quietest, deepest parts of my soul. That's why to this day, not a night goes by that I don't dream that I am there. There in my dreams, the people I encounter are the ones I lived among for the first eighteen years of my life. The words that come to me are the ones that I grew up hearing and that I grew accustomed to bantering with during those years. And even when I dream of my life here in Germany, even then the scenes are mixed in with those from home. Ultimately the ones from home dominate the cinema of my dreams. While I might dream I am in a highspeed train, it travels through the forests and villages of Zanzibar—through Pemba and Unguja.

I believe this is because *I Have a Home*. The home that lives in me, wherever I am, however I am—and that home also has me!

I HAVE A HOME, THERE IS A WE

I Have a Home

Without a home one is a slave; that will never be my fate.
I am not among such people; I have a home, there is a we.
I have a home by birth, by rearing, and in death,
Called by name Zanzibar!

I have a place, I have a people, and my people still have me.
From one mother and one father, children of one womb.
However you may count us, our numbers can't be told.
We call them Zanzibaris!

I am a child of Shengejuu, of Mwera and Mangapwani;
This is me, of Mti Mkuu, Mvimbe, and Kinazini;
It is me, of Mwanajuu, a lord of Magayani.
All of this is Zanzibar!

Anywhere I stumble, lift me back to Mikongweni.
If the place is full to brimming, drop me in Weyani.
Whether Gando whether Wete, Mwanyanya or Chukwani,
Her name is Zanzibar!

If I wander in the cities and lands of other peoples,
There's a path that I'm pursuing; I'm called to follow God.
Don't mistake me for a slave, I'm a person with a home.
By name it's Zanzibar!

Too Many

A million words I cannot speak
Are frozen on my tongue; refuse to move;
Mired . . .

Ten thousand waves I can't contain
Spread through my limbs; dawn to dusk,
I'm overtaken . . .

A thousand signs I can't point out
Appear at every bend; as I walk by,
I'm filled with sorrow . . .

A hundred acts I can't complete
Seize me up, impede my gait
It's all for you

For you, who have entrapped me
In your arms, my face uncrumples
When your name is spoken, I am saved
Oh, my country!

In the Name of My Country

In your name, I write a poem. Repeat it,
So you'll know. You, exalted, love of my heart
I have no other; none I could accept will appear
It is you, my country
Mine without question:
Mama Zinjibar!

Let me be smeared for you, I don't mind and won't be shamed
Let me be loathed, I will not falter, my heart will not despise
I will stand with you; to turn away would be impossible
I am yours
For ever and ever,
Mama Zinjibar!

Let me be cursed, I won't protest, nor will it concern me
However you are, I will embrace you; I won't turn away
I was born to you, raised in your cradle, where else would I go?
Without you
I'd have nothing to hold to,
Mama Zinjibar!

Let me be beaten, let my blood spill for you, I will be patient
Let them jail me; even if I suffer, I won't change my mind
Give me torture, it would be a blessing; I only taste sweetness
In your name
I grow fat,
Mama Zinjibar!

Let me die for you, I won't object, I will be joyful only
Let happen whatever happens; for you, I do not mind
Let me be blamed, troubles piled upon me, and chains
If I lose you,
I've nothing to hold to,
Mama Zinjibar!

She Is Called Zanzibar

Under azure skies and blazing sun
Clove trees and coconut palms, and gleaming beaches
The country of Mwinyimkuu; her name is Zanzibar

On the Indian Ocean, little slivers of land, bobbing
Waves lapping in time with the umundi drum
The land of Mwana wa Mwana; her name is Zanzibar

Kizimkazi, Msuka, Tumbatu, Fundo, and Wambaa
Names so sweet they scent the air
The land of Mkamandume; her name is Zanzibar

I love these little bits of country
in the Indian Ocean. I won't hide my love
I cling to them and won't let go; her name is Zanzibar

This green country, this gift from God
It is my tongue, my blood, my very soul
This is my greatest treasure; her name is Zanzibar

Land of the generous, the pious, and the clean
Country of the disciplined and resourceful
This place of learning, her name is Zanzibar

May you not be wiped from the face of the world
May you live, my country, until the final siren calls
Let my children come and find you
and your name still Zanzibar

The Lord Taketh

When the native is made foreign, ousted, snubbed
And the foreigner made native, sought after, blessed
Know that we are finished, over, done
Worthless, fetid, we are rotten already

Let's await the final moments when our souls are snatched away
Clothes stripped from our bodies, let our skin be washed
Let them lower down our coffins and shroud us with white cloth
Let them read our final rites; let them pack the soil down
My friend, let us be interred

Let them meet in mourning, with sweets and bitter coffee
To offer each other solace, feigning painful wails
Let them recite from one to another
Innalillahi wainna ilayhir raajiun
The Lord giveth, the Lord taketh away
To him we belong and to him we return

Receive This Tear

The heart groaned by way of the tongue
And the tongue grew tired of going unheard
Now a tear is forming, perhaps you'll accept it
Catch it before it falls

Now a tear is falling, perhaps you'll believe
I put words to paper, but when the message arrived
You refused to respond, threw it to the fire
Please now be moved to speak

Watch as it drops, slides down my cheek
reaching my chin; landing on my chest
This tear that is falling is yours, my love
Why won't you receive it?

My eye has gone soft, the lashes are wet
The lid is open, but it doesn't see
There is only you; I want nothing else
I weep the moment I remember

It's not the eye that suffers, though it makes these tears
It offers its service but alone it doesn't see
It's the heart that's uncertain, ensnared by love
Why can it not untangle?

Look how I've shriveled, like a wretched beast
Persecution shrinks me but you won't believe
I have truly become vile; value my tears
Don't let them dry up

And if it's not the right time, say so and release me
I will continue to suffer, but only deep within
I won't make a scandal, my name in the streets
Realize, please, will you realize!

I Remember

I remember, long ago, Zenj was robust
The first to see sunrise, it woke while others slept
The very measure of stability, our place was revered
Today, what is left?

I remember my Zinjibar. It was a nation
With rank, respected 'round the world,
Encircled with laurels, celebrated not chained
Today, what is left?

And so I remember—I wasn't there, but I'm told
We were able, we were present, I'm told that we were
And then, that we fell, and have yet to rise again
Today, what is left?

Our country has collapsed, and it writhes on the ground
Devastated, helpless, we ply it with herbs
But it will rise up, if we love the Most Kind, it will be again
Larger than before!

Dream

I dream I am the colonizer reigning over Europe
Germany, Switzerland, Romania, UK
All are in my hands, smothered beneath me

Scotland and Portugal, Denmark and Russia
They sit at my feet, awaiting my command
I tell them: "Fight!" In an instant, they're at war

I dream I'm on my throne, with a powerful army
The mzungu's the poor one, attired in rags
Timid and wretched, a beggar, a waif

The powerful United States: I dream it is gone
Texas, California; Florida is stunted
I grip the rudder, and the UN bows

To the south and the north, Africa and the Gulf,
Zanzibar's flag flutters on its pole
The country of my heart transformed into empire

I dream the colonies of America and Europe
Are tired of subordination, fighting to be free
They hide in the forests, plotting to overthrow me

Though my heart protests, I am forced to let them go
But still they are destitute, they struggle to rise up
I soak them with debts, and their dependence grows

Startling in my sleep, my consciousness returns
Oh. I'm on my mattress, ravaged by bedbugs
Zanzibar, imagine, its citizens run away!

It's Already in Pieces

The way it is broken, it cannot be healed
The place where it's cracked, it cannot be joined
It's already smashed and can't be reassembled
The thing is in pieces

The place it's been taken, it can't be pulled back from
The way it is stuck, it can't wriggle free
The way it was bound, it cannot be loosened
The thing's tied in knots

The way it's been dirtied, it cannot be cleaned
The way it was pierced, it'll never be patched
Where it was torn, it cannot be sewn
The thing is in tatters

The way it's gone missing, it can't be recovered
The way it's entangled, it can't be unwound
It's already crooked, it can't be set straight
The thing has been lost

The way it's been dirtied, it cannot be cleaned
The way it has fallen, it won't stand again
That which has spilled can never be gathered
The thing is already done

Your Equal

I pull out the scale, seeking your measure
But the pan plummets beneath you, your portion too grand
The other side, piled with weights, will not budge
No place proves your equal
If I die tomorrow,
let my grave be dug there

I take up my pen to write out your praises
I use up the ink and still have words
The pages run out but I still haven't finished
Arabs, Europeans, Americans have their versions,
There are plenty of volumes—
But it isn't enough
My pride overflows to be called your son

I wake early, at daybreak
And gather the people
Recite to them your glories as the sun gets high
Soon it is evening and before long, dawn
Here I still am; I've scarcely begun
The call to prayer sounds and this day also passes
I still haven't finished; no end to your charms

No other, my Zenj, can stand as your equal
Worthy of esteem, humanity's preserve
It boils my blood when your character is marred
I would rise to the sky to struggle for your freedoms
Sink into the ocean to defend your name
I won't allow your repute to be tarnished, I'll fight by any means

I'm Coming Home

Brother, I'm coming; very soon, I'm coming home
I'm coming for my parents, for the country that is ours
I'm coming to the place, you could say, that makes me human
When God wills it, I will come and nothing's in my way

I'm coming to see it all, the scarcity and abundance
Chake Chake and Wete, Pandani and Wambaa
To see my family and my people, to let them all see me
Bliss or disappointment: It is ours, whatever's there

For real, I'm coming home and the homegoer lacks nothing
I'm coming and I don't care, whatever has gone wrong
I'm coming with my mind, my education and understanding
The many I come to see, they are mine and I am theirs

I'm coming home to my elders, my father and my mother
To the place of my devotion, my pride and only treasure
Even if I'm punished, this return is what I've chosen
Whatever consequence awaits me, it's what I chose to bear

So bring greetings when you see them, to any of my kin
Tell them it's arriving soon, the time for my return
Tell them I'm resolved and not a thing can change my mind
I'm coming 'cause I've accepted who and where I need to be

I've No Choice but to Go

My heart pounds when I see you, my figure trembles
Darkness spreads itself across the world and I am numb
The heavens have frozen: birds stilled, stones upturned
It's devastating saying goodbye to you

I've no choice but to go, despite the anguish of parting
Despite my love, I must move; this is how it must be
I know I'll wither and grow weak with this weeping
How I lament saying goodbye to you

The tears defeat me, spill from their abode, and soak in
They are not tears of meanness but of a heart perplexed
This journey, though unavoidable, is a stone in my throat
If only you'd say: Don't leave me!

My heart has grown hard; it wants nothing apart from you
You've pounded it dry already; you should know
Although I am going, the swallowing wounds me
And still it is necessary, I must leave you behind

It Will End

I was thinking of those things as regret closed its grip
my heart seduced by all I'd left behind
durian and apples, rambutan and the like
radiant sun and
wide open ocean
glittering shores
when suddenly the news came . . .

Kiungoni, those bombs being hurled
Tomondo, that cascade of lead
all day those whips being lashed
that blameless blood spilled
suffering descending on my brothers—
I am no different from them, surely
if I were there, it would be me.

But there is an end . . .

Every beginning has one.
A tomorrow must come,
for here, before our eyes, is today.
Those boot-trampled rights
those children wailing
those elders in the line of fire

Triumph will be theirs.

We Have This Tree

We have this tree and we carry it carefully
But we don't want its wood, its branches or its trunk
What we want instead is to throw it to the ground
And we'd do the same to its so-called protectors

Those pretending to protect it should anticipate trouble
If they love it so much, we won't stand in the way
We'll cut them to pieces while everyone looks on
The tree will fall if they climb up or they climb down

Let them climb up or climb down, the tree will still die
We've pruned it already, axed all its branches
The first day there is sun, you'll see it shrivel up
It's a duty for us all to cut this tree down

The falling of this tree could happen any time
It's not a matter for talk, or a question of doubt
It's a matter of time, and the signs now abound
Let's watch them go on, who say they are ready

Let's watch those who say they'll hold on to the tree
Let them hold it and have it, and see if it stands
It will knock them down too and bury them in its hole
That's the ancient promise of this tree that we have

The Voice of My Country

I hear the voice of ocean waves
And rushing wind
They sing to me their poetry, a sweetness
In my ears
It comes to me by name, my country Zanzibar
"Child, come!"
I can't resist the call or withhold my reply
I go, running

If I'm called a fool for this, my country
By those who shout my name
It won't rob me of my cunning, my dignity, my grace
It's my faith
That gives me strength, shields my resolve
And love for my dear ones
Through my country I am human; for it, I am ravaged
This is nothing new!

I am ravaged, ruined for my homeland
Their talk does not concern me
I don't care what wickedness they speak
It doesn't even reach me
Nor are my words just froth; my love is lasting
For my country
Given to me by God, let me not be unworthy
This I will always have!

Don't Make Me an Orphan

Oh Baba, oh Mama, accept my tears
I am crying for peace, crying in supplication
I fear disaster at the polls
Please don't make me an orphan, don't make me a refugee

My eminent ones, I sing in memorial
I remember all that transpired
The abuse, the suspicion, the malice and violation
My fellows became orphans, others refugees

So I send you this missive, although you are my elders
Please tell those in charge, the strongmen in power
The government, the parties, the election commissions
That I don't want to be made an orphan and you won't be refugees

Tell the security units and the keepers of the peace,
From the islands to the mainland: They are tasked with your safety
With God as my witness, I'll condemn them forever
If they turn me into an orphan or make me a refugee

I'm not a senseless beast, with no thoughts in my head
I'm a child of Adam, created to have dreams
For those dreams to be realized, I have to be looked after
I won't be made an orphan or turned into a refugee

What I want is refuge, a safe place to sleep
What I want is to study, to grow and find work
And I want to reach adulthood as you have, my parents
I don't want to be left an orphan, or made a refugee

The powerful people, especially, should consider
That they too have children with dreams such as these
If they bring devastation, if the whole country mourns
They too will be orphans, they too will be refugees

Peace first and peace after, there is no greater law
However the public decides, let that be the decision
Whomever the people name should be allowed to govern
We shouldn't be made orphans or turned into refugees!

The Butterfly Fish

It's not fat, not long, has no shape or color
Just erratic and hostile and many such things
That which loves fame and gossip and power
That is indeed the butterfly fish

Purveyor of talk, sower of harm
Words without feeling, words without care
It carries them upright, pretends they're adazzle
That is indeed the butterfly fish

When caught by those wronged, it cowers in a ball
Cries out for help with its eyes full of tears
It wants to be forgiven, so it doesn't get got
That is indeed the butterfly fish

That is indeed the butterfly fish
Its job is confusion, mischief its game
I want to crush it, with curses and damnation
But the butterfly fish scarcely fills my mouth

But She Wasn't the One

When I saw how she was formed: beautiful, sparkling
My heart spilled to the floor in tiny little pieces
Even when it recovered I had no choice but to love her
Oh but I was looking for trouble

The way she was pure, her face like the moon
The way her skin shone, her movements sweet
She shimmied as she walked, I wished she'd walk forever
Oh but she was cruel

When her lips parted, grace was in her voice
The words from her mouth had the flavor of dates
I inflated her rank, to me she was Afande
Oh but it was a quagmire

I drew her to my heart to keep love from going sour
I spoke of her in my sleep till the pillows were impure
Anything she wanted, it was my pleasure to make happen
Oh but she wanted it all

Seeing that I was broken, she looked for a way out
She left me in confusion, like the child of a fool
As soon as I complained, she cut me down to size
Her words were like stones

I loved her and wanted her, so she'd want me and love me
The day my heart shattered, it was hers to mend
Instead she turned away, she wanted to do better
This is how I knew she wasn't the one

We All Have Our End

We all have our end, and it's what we fear most
Our books being closed before the final page
Our breath snuffing out before we are ready
God, may the end be good

Finishing our days, the sun hitting the horizon
We look at our children, the young we leave behind
We remember our actions and we go to God with them
We cry as we exhale

We all have our end; this one today, another tomorrow
When our eyelids are shut and darkness our only cloth
With soil poured over and pressed down from above
Generous One, receive us

When our time arrives to make that grand journey
Please make the way swift and the path unobstructed
Forgive our mistakes; let us not travel with them
And may the end be good

Zenj, My Dear

If you'd given me gold, diamonds, and rubies
And barrels of silver, and bowls of jewels
For rejecting my Zenj, I wouldn't reject her
I'm content you take everything else but not this

Zenj is my soul, my breath, my heart
She is my glory, my vaunt, my rank
Without Zenj, I have nothing, only afterlife remains
So I swear, she is with me, wherever I go

I'll boast for my lifetime, as long as Zenj thrives
If you ask me what I want, a place of fine things
Muslin, silk, and satin, I will tell you:
If I can't have my Zenj, it will never be enough

Zenj is my faith and this I don't hide
Ask who I am, I will tell you: Zanzibari
If I die, where should you bury me? The answer is Zenj
Wash these limbs
Carry my bier
My brothers, my people
Let her soil conceal me

If I die while Zenj lives, I won't yet have perished
If Zenj departs while I breathe
It will not be life,
Better I go first if Zenj must expire
I can't endure the heartbreak,
Please God take me first

How Can I Stop Crying?

I cry not for Salama, she too is God's child
My kin are not special, even the faultless die
I cry for the bitterness, the tragedy that befell her
How could she be poisoned?

I cry not for the years, the life she had left
Death comes at any moment, and we pass from this world
I cry for her struggle, for a death bound in chains
How could she be captive?

I cry not from loneliness, in this world I'm not alone
Our family will come together and gather our relations
I cry for how she suffered, for a death shrouded in shadow
How could she disappear?

I cry out with questions, yearn for their answers
I'm far from my people, far from where she was
I received their account, made sure she was buried
But how can I stop crying?

My Country Is Bereaved

My country cries, it has sunken into mourning
Her children have perished like wood in a fire
A ship has capsized in the tides of the sea
Oh God, Oh Beneficent One, bring down the cloth of patience

Bring down the cloth of patience and strength to our shoulders
So that we can bear the pain and keep from collapsing
Bring down your protection, health, and well-being
God, what calamity have your people faced?

The disaster that engulfs us is immense beyond measure
Even as we wipe our faces, there are tears yet in our eyes
They hasten to drop down, drenching our breasts
Look at the orphans, their hearts have been broken

Their hearts have been broken, these poor sweet things
Their parents have left them, now where will they go?
You are surely the only One, who can offer them comfort
And those who are injured, swiftly grant them strength

Dreams Fly

Dreams fly, they are flying, I am witness to this
They are coming and going where the stuff of dreams lives
You saw them opening like a book spread before you
So, dream, don't stop dreaming, a dream can come true

Dreams go up, they are flying, they speed up ahead
Sometimes they lie still, wait for you to catch up
If they see you are late, they might come to surprise you
They tell you: Hurry, run, it will be, it will be

Dreams can be realized, ask the experienced ones who know
Long ago the things I wanted came to me in my dreams
Not long after I sought them, I saw them, there they were
I fell to the ground, gave my praise up to God

Witness, I am witness to dreams being fulfilled
It has happened—what I dreamed has turned out to come true
Every day there are more, I see them, they're unfolding
Dream for yourself and you'll see them coming true

Dream then dream more, your dreams will be realized
Don't say it doesn't happen when you still have today
If today goes by, still, there is also tomorrow
The things that you wanted, your dreams will come true

If Nurturing Is Beyond You

The way a human is born, so it is with love
Its beginnings impure, it must be nuzzled and stroked
Its parents two souls, two hearts that have softened

Love, like a child, needs to be nurtured
And nurturing is labor, requires toil and effort
The caregivers of love are the lovers themselves

Love requires preparation, swaddling clothes
Love requires tending, treatment when it ails
Love requires care and attention to its needs

Entering into love is choosing to nurture
If you fail to respect this, your love will be spoiled
Like sickness that erupts in your head or your belly

If nurturing is beyond you, don't enter into love
You'll be taken for a dolt who lacks understanding
Your position will crumble, disgrace on your name

Greetings to My Mothers

I write this letter to you, my esteemed ones
So you receive my greetings, healthy and whole
Have no doubt for your child; I am unharmed
My constant concern is only missing you

This matter of missing is a burden that never ends
I fear you are troubled, that life isn't going well
It's been a long time, a full month since I left
Allah the Generous is the one who knows for sure

He's the one who knows when we'll see each other again
Only he, our God, Rabbuka, Subhana
But I have no doubt, the day is not far
We will hold each other's gaze and our hearts will open

Hearts will unfold, when child sees mother
I will leap in the air with impatience *Wallahi*
My tears will pour out with immeasurable joy
Oh God, Rabbana, let this promise remain.

It will not be rescinded, the promise I speak of
I will come to where you are, my beloved mothers
I will find you still healthy, not yet fatigued,
And I'll stay with you forever; I will not desert you!

Alhamdulillah

I give glory to You, my God, though I'm far
I'm far from my country, far from my own
My gratitude is limitless, there is no compare

It isn't compensation; You can't be repaid
You are the God of abundance, the King of kings
You have given me so much, riches that don't subside

Thank you for this life, for the air that I breathe
For the talents I was given, the understanding that I hold
How many do not know, Rabb, the things that I know

Thank you for the parents you chose for my birth
Thank you for the nurses who guided my growth
From them I have received a love of no equal

I am grateful to you for the house you've kept standing
For the woman I married, I could sing a chorus of praise
For the children we prayed for and by your grace were granted

The relatives you allowed me, both female and male
The siblings who came after me and the ones whom I followed
You have given me all this, Rabb, I have no words

Beyond gratitude, my God, I have nothing I can offer
To you alone, Beneficent One, let me only say this
I cherish your grace and the grace of your kingdom

May I continue to thank you for all I've been given
May I never curse your name or be unworthy of these
Allah, the All-forgiving, forgive me for my sins

What Goes Around Comes

What goes around comes, that's the way of the world
Blessed ones receive, light shines down from above
Good fortune heaps upon them that everyone can see
But luck dries up in the end and difficulties come

When difficulties come and fill Sayyids with doubt
Pride gets embarrassed and weakness overwhelms
The one who was strutting and prancing wears rags
People can be shocked when disgrace follows wealth

Spite and irritation will never change the world
Many move backward in bitterness and disbelief
Very few are firm, who aren't thrown by dismay
Turn toward the Most Loving, give thanks in defeat

To be grateful to God, this is what is called for
And to summon your own effort, don't wait to be sought
Problems have a purpose and legs are for walking
Nothing happens that isn't written, even if it's far-off

Trouble is never distant, it comes down on us all
Trouble makes no appointment, for fair weather or floods
If the wind blows warm or cold; when you're chosen, it appears
You too will know shame, what goes around comes

If You Knew That I Know

If you recognized the truth, long before today
That I know what you're up to, can name all the names
The places you go, and the friends that you have
Where would you have to alight your gaze?

You don't know that I know the sum of it all
The ones you talk to talk, tell me every last word
The moment you walk in to the seat where you sit
You have no secrets from me, so be on your guard

I know what you don't: that I already know
I leave you to boast, to shimmer like glass
In my heart I despise you, your status is scum
If you knew your position, you'd run from me fast

I swear that you'd run, if only you knew
We wouldn't be friends, you'd cast me your foe
But I keep it to myself, hold it in my heart
So continue your ways, keep thinking I don't know

Dove, I Blame You

I blame you, Dove, all this is your fault
The message of greeting you carried aloft
You come back disheveled, tell me it's lost
My love letter never arrived!

You cannot say why my hopes were dashed
Why you never delivered my note, as I'd asked
In the end you play dumb, are you cunning or daft?
Why do you make me doubt?

Dove, come now tell me, was your passage breached?
How is it you return with your task incomplete?
Did the paper burn up; did you forget?
I promise you'll come to regret!

Tears, Spill

Tears o tears, spill so I am cleansed
Torrents o torrents, make clean my heart
I can't take cannot take the tricks and machinations
The constant frustration, this is how he is!

In causing frustration, this man has no equal
He has nothing to bequeath as far as I can see
I will not forgive can't forgive what he's done
Spill then, tears, spill, so my chest might relieve me!

If You Don't Have It, You Don't Have It

You don't have what you don't have, is color sold in a can?
You were formed with this color; black is not a stain
By its nature it has worth, God gave you this face
Value your body, what do you want with whiteness?

If you don't have it you don't have it, hair can't be faked
The way you were formed is your natural shape
Don't spend all your money on potions and wigs
Calm your mind and accept your beauty as it is

You don't have what you don't have, breasts that stand up?
When you try to construct them they reject you themselves
You end up getting looks, people mock you in the street
Let what you have be enough, accept what you receive

If you don't have it you don't have it, backsides can't be made
These thighs you bulk up, they're not the same
It's not yours what you're shaking, purchased in a shop
Rather than strutting around: Love yourself, walk your talk

Release Me

Release me, unlock this cage that imprisons me inside
Take down this load that threatens to break my hip
Who if not you will save me from disaster?

Spring me from this trap, where I've grown numb in my entrapment
Let me breathe, I need air, I'm exhausted from the pacing
It is you and only you with the strength to beat all strength

It is you, my Lord, who delivers your desire upon the living
If you want something, it happens, you speak "go" and it will go
Likewise, if you don't, it will linger at the crossroads

So God please set me free from the clothing that confines me
Save me from this flood; the water has overwhelmed me
Don't leave me to be killed here; I have children at home

Wasted Soul

I know you're not mine and what's more you cannot be
I was not written for you and perhaps that's my provision
But I hold on to hope that you'll receive my words
If you'll accept it, my soul is yours

My soul is indeed yours, I say this as I know it
I know we're not aligned and perhaps never will be
My intention is not yours, our aims are not the same
I'm trying to understand, but I accept that I'm a martyr

For you I'm a martyr and I know you are aware
I can't boast that you are mine—I know that you are not
And neither can I deny that for you I've gone to pieces
Although you didn't choose me, I'm overcome with love

Love has overwhelmed me though I'm lost for words
Whatever comes now, I cannot stop loving
However far I travel, however close I come
For me it's all the same, my heart is entrapped

My heart is entrapped but I travel in prayer
If you look into the past, if you draw out your recollections
You will find me standing there, with arms outstretched
Ready to receive you, if only you were to choose

The day that you choose me, that I should be your cure
Know that I won't refuse, nor will I protest you
Know that I accepted you from the first rising of the sun
Even if that sun sets, I can never reject you!

A Pot Won't Lack for Soot

The pot spends all day cooking tubers and roots
From first light of dawn till nightfall it works
You can't blame a pot for being covered in soot

Why the petty words, when you know its condition?
It's a woodstove, no less: fueled by splinters and twigs
A pot with its belly in the coals does not glisten

The blackness of its bottom doesn't mean it's no good
It's the mark of persistence, adversity overcome
Perched all day on the fire, a pot won't lack for soot

These Days I've Matured

I don't cry anymore, I've matured these days
Whatever happens to me, I figure is my size
I've resolved to go along without dropping tears
I go to sleep and it's there when I open my eyes

I go to sleep and it's there when I open my eyes
Facing north facing south, daybreak or dusk
I run alongside it and don't lose any time
It doesn't give me pleasure but I fall with it and rise

I fall with it and rise, like an ant, I carry on
I accept what is planned, the destiny I've been thrown
No matter what is said, words are not stones
My load-bearing heart can shoulder it all

My capable heart can stand these trials
It's not the same heart that I carried before
The one that cried out with tears and denials
Today it is bold, ready for what comes

What was too much before I'm now ready to confront
Ready to stop stammering, no longer unsure
In the past when I was struck, I shattered like glass
These days I have matured, I don't cry anymore

We People of This World

By name, we are told, we are children of Adam
With haughty heads that care little for restraint
Our love is blunt and our actions are senseless
Grumbling, starting fights, many of us are unwhole

We are obstinate like goats with ropes 'round our necks
If we resolve to do a thing, even leap down a shaft
We take no advice, no matter who gives it
We are many in this world, people like goats

We are blind like centipedes without eyes on our faces
Even with mirrors, we don't see who we are
Only when we collide do we believe a thing is there
God what kind of people are we, in this world

Our haste is like frogs, we've no patience for another
We are careless with each other, we use might over mind
The result is only loss, we can never see a profit
Without a scrap of wisdom, we've all become brutes

We crash when we encounter another on the road
We run like we're in drills, like horses in a race
Run after some task that scarcely enters the mind
Shove like bad spirits though our shape is human

And that is how it is, people acting like beasts
And that is indeed our world, low in esteem
Where do we lay our hopes, and toward what turn our faces?
Though we feign innocence, we too are at fault

When You Fear People You Don't Act

However much you want to act, fear of people can prevent you
People's ways can be provoking, their meanness and their spite
If they see you're getting plump, they ask why you aren't starving
Insult you for failing to starve, if they see you're getting plump

When you succeed in doing things, they refuse to see success
If you leave things and let them spoil, then they label you a flop
They'll say look how you've spoiled it, how little you belong
They themselves do nothing, but they don't want you to act

The place you fear to go, they'll ask: Why don't you go there?
Sometimes pointing a finger, other times rattling a drum
Ultimately they spin a story with things that never happened
They'll say to a crowd: "This person doesn't act!"

If you sound a call to action and request that they join you
They'll freeze in their positions, not one will make a move
But if you act on your own, "So you think you are better?"
When you fear this you won't act, too afraid to do a thing

So given you're a doer, what do you wait for by not doing?
Given you're an actor, what do you wait for that you don't act?
Given that you're a maker, don't worry about the talk
If you fear all that you won't and if you can act, you should

Where Are They?

I'm pondering the old ways, what I used to see around us
I search but cannot find them; where exactly have they gone?
Neither hearts nor eyes contain them; the habits of today
Are nothing like the old ways; where has it gone, that forgotten time?

Extending kindness to each other has become a foreign practice
Much more common now to quibble and look to pick a fight
It seems that even goodness is a thing of yesteryear
I look at today's people: They don't even wish to have it

Hearts devoid of reverence, gratitude in crumbs
Humans who criticize one another populate the world
What does goodness even mean for those who hand out trouble?
Ya Illahi Ya Rabbana, what has seized your people?

Very few out on the field are searching out their brothers
The majority are vicious, tearing into each other like meat
Where are they who reach for the shoulder of another
Alas, I can no longer find them, I dream them in a dream

I long to see the old days
A world of peace, of joy and love
A world of satiety and faith, and people with respect
Instead I'm told that's past; this is the modern age

Get Caught and Remember Me

I put a curse on you now in the name of the one you cursed
You who would play games with a person full of love
Let God overcome your scorn and may it come back upon you
You, depraved one, you

Get caught and remember me, my name on your lips
Let sleep refuse to come, and your pillows soak with tears
Call for me and get nothing, let me never send you greetings
You, foolish one, you

Find a rude and arrogant person, someone like yourself
A cruel and insolent ogre, and let the brute rip out your soul
May you find a ruthless oaf, not a weak person like me
You, ill omen, you

Find yourself a creature with a gaping maw and tongue
A person with so many words, they can outlast even you
A mouthy troublemaker who was cut off by his mother
You, arrogant one, you

May this little prayer not falter, may God receive my words
May yearning grip your body and refuse to let you go
May it knock you to the floor and thrust you back to standing
You, rude thing, you

My prayer is that you're caught, captured in a cage
Regretful and disgraced, your name on every tongue
And finally may you fall, a beggar at our feet
May you plead to be taken in

Choke on your own breath as you come and cry my name
Let me be the one to pour insults and humiliation
Till the very end when I hold you and pity overtakes me
Only then will I forgive

The World Isn't Pleasure

This world isn't level, it bends as it rises
Not flat, open plains but forests and bush
Even the weather never stops changing
To give then take away is the state of the world

Joyful days don't come without uncertainty behind them
They can't all be happy, sorrow is also there
There are days filled with fury, others with laughter
Healthy days and ill; that's the state of the world

There is that which is whole and that which is rotten
There are people who talk and those who respond
Not everyone who acts wholesome has pure intentions
One prays, one performs; that's the state of the world

Don't lose heart, then, listen: Problems will find us
We won't die in pleasure but we won't die of doubt
This is how the world is, days go up and come down
You get out, you come in, that's the state of the world

Neither is it suffering for years on top of suffering
Where there's remembrance and faith, blessings will return
There are those who deny and others who believe
Evil and righteousness, that's the state of the world

Let my pen be still now, let this word be finished
And you, get prepared to take on what comes
When the doubts come, be patient, don't throw yourself down
He seems one way but he's another, that's the state of the world

Popobawa Has Returned

Here is Popobawa, after its break, back to torment us
People are haunted, minds cursed and taunted; the beast forcing its will
Back to its antics, it wreaks nothing but havoc, constant aggravation
It wanted to kill us and it would with a quickness, if only it was able
But the one who makes choices about what destroys us is God, not some creature
We don't fear such problems, however much it hounds us, it can't take our lives!

It can't take our lives, no matter what it tries with its plagues of destruction
For our side, we know: Any time it could go, pack its bags up and leave
And we will remain, through dry season and rains, it won't rule our land
It will fly round, make demands, grow tired and land, exhausted from its harassment
By God's strength, 'twill collapse and cease its attacks, fall useless from the sky
We aren't afraid of struggle, though it may give us trouble, it can't take our lives!

Isolation Cradles

Isolation is suffering—it is anguish and desolation
Isolation wraps you up, and it cradles you toward death
Isolation, without a friend, is more than pain, it's illness
You'll try out every cure without knowing your disease

Isolation is disconnection from those who know you well
Their words become disturbance, the stories they begin to tell
And this is the worst heartache, you find yourself possessed
In isolation you're alone, not a single person is yours

Isolation is to be reviled, people discriminate against you
You're the target of their cruelty, words bent on your undoing
You sit down by yourself, tears coming on like rain
Against a life of being shunned, death would be your choice

Generosity Won't Be Repaid

Do for a person what brings contentment
Sprinkle him with flattering words till he's appeased
Spoil him and feed him, fulfill his every need
But don't forget he's human, gratitude is rare

If you give him your own supper and he throws it to the floor
Even then: Protect him, call to him by name
Elevate his status, crown him with your praise
Gratitude is difficult, it's best for you to know

He could be your brother, closest of your kin
When you do things to bring him closer
Love in such a way that he can feel no want
Remember he is human, he will not pay you back

It's an old truth about humanity that gratitude is rare
Payment for good deeds is a habit of the heart
This is the way it was and the way it will always be
It's uncommon for a person to be thankful for what he receives

Carry out your deeds but seek approval from only One
He alone will pay, the most glorious of payments
If you wish for something more, you'll get nothing but frustration
To be generous with humans is to take the longest view

Little Half My Heart

I say goodbye today, sweet apple of my eye
The journey I embark on is not a thing you wanted
So I give you this to stay with: this little half my heart
Do with it as you will, to you I hand it over

I hand it over to you, to do with as you like
It's yours and yours alone, you won't be forced to do a thing
Nor will you be held to blame, no matter how you choose
Even if your decision harms this little heart

If you harm this little heart, quietly or in the open
And the ones who do not know you come ascribing blame
I will come and tell the gossips to stop what they are saying
You shouldn't be responsible for that which is your right

It is yours, this little half, and yours the right to choose
This little half my heart, if you want to hold it close
Keep it close for all your life, and do with it as you will
Although I have my hopes, you can do no wrong

Giving and Receiving

Don't say it's the rich who gave alms
Their money heaped in piles around them
Giving comes not of power but of faith
You are supposed to already know this

It's not just ascetics who received
Some were even reigning emirs
They were willing to accept what was given
They received without resistance or pride

The gifts might not have been cars
Silk finery or garlands of bay
Maybe it was a spoonful of sugar
That was the limit of their alms

And neither were the receivers insulted
To be given such meager gifts
Instead they humbled themselves
and asked to be given grace

It's the giver who chooses the gift
A receiver should not be so brazen
For both it is reverence that compels them
And reverence is always allowed

Bequest

My child, as my bequest, I give you what I have
It has no worldly weight, measured on the scale
Lift it to your head whenever you feel able,
Don't lean on other people; they will only vex you

My child, just one spark is enough to start a blaze,
A scorching conflagration that burns down to the ground
We could dry up every river extinguishing what we've begun
Mind the embers in your heart; do not fan the flames

The sky may look clear and shiny but
The road winds and makes sharp turns
Not all who dress in wool spin the thread themselves
Very few things are solid; the world is upside down

Calm yourself, my child, do you need your name to be known?
Top is bottom; bottom, top; the world is not the same
You're on earth and not in heaven; you haven't yet been saved
You cannot be an angel, but don't make yourself from jinn

A tempest wind is blowing, things are falling that were still
Things that once were steady swirl above our heads
My child, you should duck, if you must, lie on the ground
If you set your mind to it, there's nothing that can't be done

Learn to repair what's worn, you'll always find new uses
Even a rotten fruit doesn't deserve to be thrown away
It has a right to be planted and the ground around it wetted
From there a tree might sprout, from which new fruit are born

I foresee where we're headed and fear the worst to come,
The most righteous kinds of behavior may be seen as terrible things
Respect will be taboo as violence becomes the norm
So dear child, please be careful, let learning be your companion

My child, I won't stop naming wrongs when I see them in the world
Though as you grow and live, you'll recognize more and more
You'll see they are like smoke, they gather then they clear
Be careful leaning against it, the world is a dry tree

Be Tolerant

I see what's happening to you, your agitation and doubts
It's eating you alive, you've aged beyond your time
I see the state you're in; I know how you suffer
Don't feel isolated, sister, you're not alone

You can handle this condition, even if you're confused
But listen to your brother, hear what I have to say
Right now many things are coming at you at once
We have to stand up quickly to take them all on

My sister, harden your heart, turn your face toward God
What afflicts you isn't new; you're not the first to suffer
This is how the world is, very little laughter
But plenty to give us doubts, plenty to make us cry

The things that have happened have happened as they were planned
Yesterday you were fleeing, feeling there was nowhere to go
And today new things have sprung up, before the rest moved on
I know you're feeling pain, but swallow down your cries

Swallow down your cries, don't make yourself unwell
Persevere through the difficulty, make your way across
You can handle what is happening, all of this will end
We are not yet angels, sister, we still have work to do

Lastly, know you're not alone, I'll say this again
You and I are together, I share in all your worries
Everything that happens, I'll be here by your side
In all that I have written, I will always be your brother

This Is How I Am

Sometimes I'm a dove, sitting in a palm
Content to be a plaything, tame and unperturbed
I land right in their hands, walk across their shoulders
Many expect this of me; this is how i am

Sometimes I'm a peacock, confident and proud
Fancy myself ample, flawless and complete
Ignore the ones beneath me, tail high in the air
Arrogant and flashy; this is how i am

When I'm feeling duck-like, I shout a mighty quack
Though I'm focused on devouring, it does not garner fear
I dabble in the muck to find the things I seek
Its not everyone who knows this; but this is how i am

Sometimes I'm a cat, guardian of the home
I know every creature that enters and every one that leaves
I attack whoever makes trouble, roaches and mice beware
My stomping ground's the kitchen; this is how i am

But I can also be a lion, with a vicious roar and bite
If I get angry and bristle, the entire plain will hush
They fear I might attack them or come destroy their homes
For this reason I am dreaded; this is how i am

Or perhaps I am a chameleon, this is what you tell me
That I put on a different demeanor whenever I feel the need
For a human it's nothing special, it's a habit we all have
I know we both know this; how I am is how you are

When a New Thing Becomes a Wound

At first people were soothed; the shiny new thing aglow
A beautiful thing with flowers and a loveliness of form
Every eye was drawn to it and every heart fell in love
But lo, it's already swollen and I think it's beginning to smell

The new thing has started stinking; it's rotting from the inside
But nobody knows where it came from and no one will claim it as theirs
Now there is no newness, all that's left is a sore
But we all sit and chew on leaves: "How did this come to be!?"

"Why has this come to be," is the question on every mouth
We wish to know how it happened
That a new thing becomes a wound
From the moment it arrived, the wrapping hasn't been removed

Since it was first presented, it just sits there without moving
Time hasn't taken it away and it's already become too much
We all plug up our noses, in the face of the spreading stink
The love we had has melted, we feel a deep shame in our hearts

In our hearts we feel ashamed by how sick we were with love
The one who brought it has cursed us, to avoid the curse himself
The rest of us leave it alone, given how things have gone
When a new thing becomes a wound, everyone seems to grow weak

The Choice That Can't Be Chosen

It's not offered to me out of meanness, nor is it out of disdain
Nor am I in a hurry, I am peaceful and perfectly still
And I am not a buffoon, I know what it is I was offered
I'm told that the choice is mine
But even with all of this
My heart simply refuses
Because every choice is a yes, I cannot decide on one

My heart simply refuses, it cannot make a choice
It cannot find one that falls short
Nor one that's especially pleasing
For my heart, each appears worthy, so it cannot lay one aside
And the thing that really pains me
I won't be allowed to have both
I'm forced to make a choice; I know I won't be given two

I won't be left to take them, one first and then the other
Only one of these is for me, whichever one I choose
"The other is for your fellow"—this is what I'm told
I hesitate and stutter, pick one up then put it down
One moment yes it is this one
The next I am not so sure
And this is my condition when I decide to reject them both

Life Is Love

We are formed of love, not of envy or greed
Our bodies have been sculpted, love the very clay
The love itself is God's, of community and faith
What we hope for doesn't come when we slander love

If people learned to foster it, love could be a cherished cure
It could solve all their conundrums, uncoil all their knots
In love there is no status—one over another
Kinship built on love can exceed all bounds

Where have the wise ones gone who refused to let it in?
Who scorned the very idea as if they had no hearts themselves?
They've now become deceivers, walking around without it
Their lives are simply sorrow, those who reject love

This is my defense of love—this poem a proclamation
And it's not simply a delusion; I'm still in my right mind
I stand for it out of tribute to the love that I remember
We can find it still among us, even if it's hard to see

Come, you who harbor love, I implore you to bring it forward
Come with it tied in ribbons, wrapped up in our hearts
Let's love each other as siblings, let hate not be our supper
Hurry, let's waste no time, let's build up our stores of love

My Khadhira, Hush Now

Khadhira, I didn't want this and I feel no yearning for it
Without another choice, one does what has to be done
I take you by the shoulder, then, to say what can be said
Though destinations may be chosen, I'm not the chooser of things
Rather, if it was written
That this be the day I leave
Then it's God's will that has said it and I'm helpless to intervene

Khadhira, please don't cry or heave your laments down
Restrain the streams of tears from spilling to the ground
Don't cause yourself such suffering, wailing in such a form
My dear, please see it plainly: Where there is departure, there is return
I swear to the Almighty
That I absolutely cannot
Live apart from my love; that's an impossible condition

Don't be so lonely, Khadhira, so miserable in this moment
That you resist what we've been handed, for we are fated beings
The impossible becomes possible, but only within measure
Don't pound your chest or stay up sobbing
Ruffling your hair
Be still, my love, be still
Since my birth, I've never left you

Khadhira, it's not unusual and you are not the first
The same thing has happened to others on the other side of the world
How could we have predicted that these things would come to you
Bitter suffering and retribution; they were afflicted with the same

Every city with such problems
Has emptied very slowly
But that's not what I'm doing, it's an intention I do not have

Khadhira, this journey I embark on
Don't think I am uprooting, disappearing from your view
I do not go by choice, but out of obligation
So accept, my love, accept; let me go now with your blessing
Then listen to me closely
This voyage will return
No matter what I find there, I won't turn my back on you

Khadhira, this I swear: I carry in my heart
To the place where I am going, every fondness, all my love
You know how you are valued; it's difficult to live without you
I do not twist my tongue, I won't turn against my word
I don't speak what I don't believe
Oh my love, my dearest,
I love you for your faith, please love me too for mine

We Will Arrive

The journey has dragged on, and we'll be late to arrive
It wasn't insignificant, the way it was thought
It was full of discomforts, worries, and doubts
   But we will arrive

It turned out to be elastic, every day stretching longer
It demanded of us greatness, humanity, education
And many of us are weak, too easily changed
   Even so, we'll arrive

The narrative has shifted, it's not the way they said
At the start the road was true, crossing was nearly certain
Which is why people in droves came together to join the crowd
   With expectations of arriving

But it turned out the way was muddy, difficult to pass
Filled with fearsome brambles and marauding men
Rarely did suffering pass us and safety offer greeting
   But we want to arrive

So the way ahead isn't level, it rises and it falls
And the season is one of suffering, not sunshine but rain
For many the journey doesn't suit, however we might want it
   Let's not hesitate, we will arrive

We should be hopeful, not despairing
We're still here, though some are missing,
We should face the distance, move on with caution
   I believe we will arrive

How Can You Drink the Sauce First?

The world is just as it's been from the very beginning
But people aren't the same in their speech or their manner
And changes of this magnitude prompt one to ask questions
How can you drink the sauce first and eat the rice after?

Not noisily or with fanfare, but the questioning should travel
Let it make its way through Msuka and settle in Mkele
Where people fill up plenty, and drink their sauce in bowls
Why do it in that order, and not have it the other way?

Although the practice has been around since much earlier times
The drinkers were not many, who drank the sauce first
Now every child and parent, each with his own ladle
Do you see them being praised for eating the rice dry?

Even the vendors in the market, now this is how they do it
All the customers who go in are first given something to drink
Sauce poured to overflowing, and only after, the second plate
How come and what is missing, that the sauce should precede the rice?

Let me tell you how it is, with the sauce poured over the rice
The ball of food in your palm is flowing over with honey
Over the edges of your fingers come golden droplets of ghee
Why wouldn't you eat that way, if you have both sauce and rice?

To do the second thing first is to separate twins when they're born
Is it some custom or an illness, or a return to older ways?
I'm calling out to the spirits, please tell me what is going on
Why would you put the sauce first, and then finish by eating rice?

The Hot Sun of Night

It was night and bitter cold
The air was calm, and the air cutting
And we, beneath the ceiling, were shivering fiercely
And that's when it happened, that nighttime sun

The hot sun of night, that's when it happened
The cocks took on the task of crowing before their time
Those who would pray prayed, thinking it was morning
No one knew any better, until we felt that hot sun

When we felt it heat up, that was when we knew
That what had dawned was the night sun, not the sun of the day
It came in through the ceiling, spreading out its rays
The cold took its leave, and the sun warmed us well

It warmed us quite well, the rays that came out
We gave thanks to Qahhar for this caretaking sun
It is all by his order, whether coldness or heat
But in the end it wasn't good, the sun began to harm

The sun began to harm, though at first we thought it good
The heat became intense and blessing turned to trouble
The ceiling got hotter and the sweat began to spill
Disease began to spread alongside the fierce sun

Alongside the fierce sun, disease began to spread
The air became dangerous, skin spots and fleas
We began to better understand the cold and its trouble
We called out to God, please Rabb reduce the heat

Please Rabb reduce the heat, we called out to God
So that the house is not an oven, baking us inside
Before dawn, let the sun begin its return journey
This night sun is too harsh—we don't want to be scorched

Peacock in a Cage

You are beautiful in shape, your every trait is pleasing
You have this desirable feature, and that one, and more
You've been given that form, those shimmering colors
These myriad hues your pride and decoration

Colors of every kind like ornaments across your body
The deepest of black, white, and red are all there
It is your very nature, this mélange of color
Let me tell you the truth: Your adornment draws me near

But the intrigue is not only the colors of your body
It's the manner of your movements, the way you take each step
The style with which you saunter is yours and yours alone
Your gestures are exquisite, your grace astounds my heart

In spite of all this, peacock, my dear, I'm feeling pain
You are locked up in a cage, your food slipped through the grate
Your movements are trapped inside, you're forbidden to step out
Peacock, you are praised, don't you want your freedom?

The beautiful visions that come to you in your sleep
That astound you with their vividness and bring hope to your heart
I only see as problems, peacock, if you are in prison
As long as you're locked up, how will they ever come true?

Despite your beautiful colors, the endless praise you receive
From morning to night you're still trapped inside
You don't have free movement and you don't have free will
Why don't you take a stand and come out of this hole?

There's No Growing Weary of Getting

Every time we receive, we desire more, we never fill
We hide yesterday's spoils, let them pile up behind closed doors
To see a thing is to want it, even if it can't be had
Handed heaven here on earth, we wouldn't hesitate to ask for more
             We never tire of getting

We wake up with this hunger, it has no stage of life or time of day
Relentless in our pursuit, even when what we want is out of reach
We prefer to drag ourselves along, break our backs till it is gotten
We only want again, still bound by thirst, even once we have
             We can never get our fill

Our quarrel is not with getting but with being forced to share
When it comes to dividing the spoils, there is deceit and tug of war
Because the moment we receive, here come the masters to take their cut
When they come to divide it up, disputes arise and they want more
             We don't quarrel with the getting

The wealthy gnash their teeth, gobbling up whatever they can find
They drag their profits behind them, pumping hands in congratulation
When those of us who do the work stand up, we're shouted down
And if we manage to gain a little, they want to take that from us too
             They never grow weary of getting

They provoke our regret, sow discord to keep us divided
The ones who had been searching start to see that there's no point
Because even when we get, dignity transmutes to greed
So better identify the gluttons, pause and ask: what more do they need?
             Let them seek for themselves

Or better yet, let's shake them off, remove the takers from among us
Once they're cleared out we work together and finally start to trust
So whatever it is we get, we distribute fairly, no longer cheating
This country: It could sparkle, stop moving backward, earn a name
We'll have truly gained

Love Is in the Tease

The secret of love's pleasure
Love's pleasure is in the tease
Not in tears or freezing up
Stiffness in the cold
Instead, it is found in play
Instead, it is found in play, measured and alluring
This is the essence of love—it's all found in the tease

Stagnancy is forbidden
It's forbidden to sit too still—a love like that will languish
Devoid of any sweetness
Devoid of sweetness and passion; neither ripe nor fully mature
A love without restraint
A love without subtle restraint simply has no craft
And restraint is in the tease

Let the sugar soften
Let the sugar soften and disperse, with a little salt thrown in
So just in case of emergency
In an emergency, it can be licked
Love is like a circle
When you step in, it's not to sit around
Its entry fee is the tease

Love is in the arousal
The pleasure of being aroused
It is never in confusion
Nor doubt nor denial of need

Love is an awakening
An awakening and a stirring, the heightening of desire
And desire is in the tease

Without teasing,
Without play,
It is flimsy, love's unable to ascend
It has no place to settle
No place to settle so it only dangles

Suddenly it races
Suddenly it's on the chase
The medicine is in the tease

Shoes Come in Pairs

This world isn't all bad, but it's not all good either
We'll never have our fill, though it's not always sweet
It's the residents of the world who truly make it bitter
Shoes come in pairs, but people wear only one

They wear only one and abandon the second
Lace up the left while rejecting the right
Still they expect praise on account of being clever
It's true foolishness, I tell you, going barefoot on one side

To go barefoot on one side is the opposite of decorum
It humiliates the wearer and shouldn't be allowed
Wearing one shoe only? This must be impudence!
It's an abasement of the feet and painful to move about

Painful to move about and an invitation for accidents
Even walking itself becomes a kind of wrath
With one foot on the road and the other in the weeds
Like indigents or paupers, they limp their way around

Instead of walking normally, they would take on a limp
The journey takes a turn before they've even begun
The feet've become accustomed to wearing a full pair
This is the troublesome thing about wearing only one

You wearers of one, you should question your choices
You brought it on yourselves, but advice's for the uncounseled
Let me tell you right now: You should always wear both shoes
To roam around in the dirt is to ask for swollen feet

Their Country, Their Tongue

It will cost you to go to a country, without speaking the people's tongue
You'll find yourself surrounded, shame heating up your face
Overwhelmed and in confusion, shedding pounds despite good health
Before you know what you're saying, you find yourself locked up

Locked up without wrongdoing, save the crime of not speaking their tongue
You're unable to catch a word, in writing or conversation
You find yourself in disaster, unable to fight your way out
Your worries eat away at you, like a chick tossed from the nest

Like a chick left by its mother, you soil yourself in fear
You will your lips to open, but your tongue swells in your mouth
In this state of utter confusion your eyes can only stare
You pray for your end to come or time to fly away

You long for time to go quickly, for the day to come to an end
It's problem on top of problem, nuisance on top of disaster
You don't know where to begin in trying to make your case
What could possibly save you from the predicament you're in?

When you encounter a problem and you cannot speak their tongue
The worries that follow are boundless, they can scarcely be written down
At times you collapse to the floor and can't find a way back up
But these issues will glide right past you, when you find you have their tongue

Home O Home

Thoughts, o thoughts, you grab my mind
This is no game, no game, these anxieties and doubts
Calm, where is the calm, let it come that I can rest

Home, o home, our place how I remember you
In the dark, here in the dark, the tears come falling down
Why, o why, did I ever go away?

Loneliness, o loneliness, cloaks me like a shroud
It kills me this, it kills, and soon I will be buried
If only, if only, I were able to escape

Solitude, o solitude, I am the child who sits alone
Steam, hot steam, that builds and scalds my gut
Let it out, let it out; I vomit up my cries

Germany, o Germany, where have you taken me?
What could you have that Zanzibar lacks?
If only, if only, I fall down in regret

Hope, o hope, I'm calling you, answer me
In my heart, deep in my heart, please find a place to settle
Don't betray me, don't betray, and take away my peace

The Pens Should Roam

The pens should roam all over, seeking truth and witness
Hopping wire fences, discovering the way things are
They should name it for the world, speaking only truth
They should never write deceit

The pens should sit on councils and listen for corruption
Keep an ear out for the grift; sort truthtellers from the crooks
The pens should censure grifters and keep them from the public
They should never spread such things

The pens should know the bootlickers, find them, and ignore them
Depend on them for nothing, know no truth can be found there
Such filth only causes hives, they should not accept their stories
The pens should turn away

A Broad-Shouldered Man

A broad-shouldered man doesn't boast, he awaits the praise of others
He who boasts is like a speck of dust, wafting around in the wind
He imagines he's a cockerel, when really he's the egg

A man of size doesn't strut, though he also can't be strutted over
Strutting is a sin, the kind of act that can't be forgiven
He doesn't strut out in public, out of desire to be feared

A real man isn't lazy, he's not a scavenger for scraps
He's willing to pitch his camp and hunt for his own game
When the time comes round for dancing, he's already made his catch

He who brags is only a braggart, and he only fools himself
His gossip is for nothing, he wants what he doesn't have
He who boasts is like a speck of dust, wafting around in the wind

Don't Desert Your Camp

It's the pride of one's belonging to dread abandoning camp
What is home is always home, however overgrown with brush
The one who knows what's his, even burdened, does not depart
How can you leave untended land when there's tending left to do?

Don't desert the path to your homestead; it led you to where you are
It was a terrible fight, but what transpired has now passed
Fence posts and pestles, amid pounding and grinding
My brother, that is our place, it's where we were raised

He's a slave who has no homeplace, to be a stranger is an ordeal
Just ask those who wander, who have no headboard behind their heads
Our lot is not their lot, praise be to our exalted God
You and I have a place that's ours; when we call out, it answers!

A sailor might move to the stern, but to the bilge he always returns
And so it is with us, though we're here, still making our way
This wandering may continue but it's not a lasting condition
A day will come that it ends, let's return then to our camp

I Am Yours

Yours, I'm only yours, I belong to no one else
Yours when you awake, sleepless through the night
Yours when you go quiet, stilled without a whisper
Yours where I am now and wherever else I go

This is me, your ear, attentive when you speak
This is me, your mouth when your ear has opened up
This is me, your light when the darkness falls upon us
And this is me, your cloth whenever you feel cold

I'm yours and only yours in all things, on all occasions
This is me, your laugh, and if needed, I'll be your wail
This is me, your joy, though I can also be your pain
Since the beginning, through the ages, this is me and I am yours

I Don't Need a Spectacle

Eye, you are the observer, see what can be observed
If you really are a seer, look out for what can be seen
Don't be an inspector, even when it cries for inspection
I don't want you to seek out spectacle; that is not what I need

Nose, you are the sniffer, sniff what is there to be sniffed
If you are an exhaler, exhale what is ready to be let go
But if you are the inhaler, let air be all you draw in
More than that becomes spectacle, and that is not what I need

Tongue, you are the taster, taste all that's here to be licked
Truly you are a speaker, speak that which needs to be said
But don't be an insulter, not even for those who deserve it
The day you do that it's a spectacle, and that is not what I need

Heart, you are a confessor, confess what weighs on your soul
Even if you are a lover, love what offers itself to be loved
Do not become a hater, even of things abhorrent
Hate is not your task—it's a spectacle and not what I need

Mind, you are the muser, muse on what comes to be mused
You are indeed the master, take me to where I must go
But I do not want confusion, no chaos-makers for me
What is right is the way forward, and a spectacle's not what I need

Take Advice

Why do you get so angry, flopping around?
Why do you fret, restlessly shifting?
Do you wait for what hasn't come?
You wish for what's not for wishing
What you hope for brings despair
Oh living being
Take advice
You will suffer

Why do you borrow what can't be repaid?
Do you go where isn't for going?
Do you want what shouldn't be wanted?
You believe what can't be believed
You lose your faith for no reason
Oh living being
Be calm
You will be stained

Do you lift what should not be raised?
Do you love what cannot be loved?
Do you sow what will never thrive?
When the sun sets you lie awake
Your problems waste you away
Oh living being
Let it be enough
You'll be a scandal

Do you trap what cannot escape?
Do you wash what can never dry?
Do you curse what can't be cursed?
I know what has burrowed in your heart
It's a terrible task, digging it out
Oh living being
Have some respect
You will bring shame

Do you laugh at what will never be funny?
Do you reply to what earns no response?
Do you dream of what cannot be gotten?
What isn't yours, since long ago
For your thirst, you will be destroyed
Oh living being
Be satisfied
You'll be deformed

Do you start what cannot be finished?
Do you pull at what cannot be pulled?
Do you think what should not be thought?
Though in your soul, it has already fastened
As your own worth dwindles away
Oh living being
Pay attention
You will act in error

Do you stretch up to where can't be reached?
Do you sit where is not meant for sitting?
What do we say that can even be said?
That you'll put trust in what can be trusted
Don't betray your faith for the unworthy
Oh living being
Rest
You will get tired

This Is How They Are

If they need to laugh, they pretend to frown
Their faces wrinkle, and they grit their teeth
Their hearts fly off with no place to settle
In their souls they rejoice, in their eyes only tears

What they want the most is what they must say no to
Bustle around like a beast eats its young
They suffer meanwhile and grumble complaints
The trouble they cause sucks everyone in

Longing to leave, they cross their legs tightly
"It smells bad outside, I don't want to see you"
Turns out they are yearning and their eyes can't rest
Even as they smile, they hide their true thoughts

A huge issue for them is made out to be nothing
Pretending instead that molehills are peaks
The one who has nothing claims to have something
Whenever he has it, he claims he does not

They are not angels, but neither are they jinn
But this is the truth of their place, not an imitation
When a parent dies, he leaves habits to his child
People come and go, but these things haven't changed

The Way I Love You

The way I love you, Zanzibar
I cannot love your peer
  nor am I ready

The way I love you, birthland
No other love can match
  and never will

The way I love you, nation
No equal will emerge
  that I'd reject you

The way I love you, kingdom
Like light on glass, it glints
  and never dulls

The way I love you, country
Take it all and more
  I won't refuse you

The way I love you, city
I'll love with every waking
  It only grows

Today's Eater, What Does He Eat?

Sure, today he eats, but what is it he's eating?
Will he eat sputum from a broken dish and a spoonful of sand?
The dregs of last night's meal and vomit from the bin?
We must ask what he is eating, even if he eats

Even if today he eats, at lunch or at supper
Look at what's in the bowl; is this your source of pride?
The stink that fills the air—how does he even swallow?
We must ask what he is eating, is it humility or bluster?

With all the fuss and swagger, we're distracted by commotion
Turns out the thing he's licking is the drool from his own lips
If this is what he's proud of, this meal—what do we call it?
Can this even be called food? Has he seen what others eat?

Has he seen what others eat, to know this thing called eating?
Has he met those who understand a meal and how it looks
Food that's cooked at home by cooks who know their culture
Today's eater just opens his mouth and pops in whatever's there

Had It Been Knowable

If only I had known that this was indeed the journey
I wouldn't have bought the ticket, I would have counseled myself first
I never would have decided to board that vessel

Had it been knowable, how far I was going
I would have taken some savings, some money and food
To avoid running out before I reached a destination

If I could've known, if I'd known that there were prowlers
That convoys would be ransacked, all their wealth poached
I'd have bought a gun and carried a machete

It wasn't something I could have known, to make my way with care
That what I'd chosen was a difficult journey
I thought I'd close and open my eyes and find I'd arrived

Because of all that has happened, the journey already begun
Though I didn't understand its difficulty and danger
There is no going back, I forge onward with zeal

Whatever should happen, however the path unfolds
I will put my chest forward, face it with courage
What is upended I will right, unless my soul should depart

Given that I'm here, I don't dream of reversal
Turning back will not heal me, that would not befit a man
When a man makes a decision, his conscience must be fulfilled

For Whom Do You Wear It?

I am asking those who wear Ramadan hijab
Who pull down their veils so they won't be seen
God-fearing for today, for today like angels
For whom are these clothes, please explain it to me

Let me ask the daughters: Do they know themselves well?
As we push past each other all year in the streets
Bodies out in the open, tiny tops and miniskirts
The photos that they post for others to see

The whole year they walk the streets
Tight clothes squeezing their bodies
How is it that today, you hide under hijab
Who do they perform for, these days of Ramadan?

If this is indeed the moon that lasts thirty days
In no time it will be over, it will leave us again
What of your respect, then, will it wait another year?
And if this is not the case, will you cover yourself again?

I see things for what they are, you are kidding yourselves
If deep in your hearts, you don't believe in covering up
If only during fasting do you rush to your closets
Remembering to veil today, is that what is called faith?

This is not an oath, my sisters, it is not conviction
And it is not respect for the month of Ramadan
This behavior is malice, you offend the Beneficent
If you have faith, wear it every day!

My Children, Forgive Me

My children, today I call you, come to me quickly
My body is drenched in sweat
I dreamed tonight of things gnawing at my heart
When I think of them
Fear grips me
What possessed me to uproot you?

At home you'd already sprouted, your roots had begun to spread
And I came and dug you up, violently ripped you out
And brought you here to a life in a foreign place
What was I seeking?
And what good will it do you?
I'm afraid I'll come to regret, that I'll be the one to blame

That you'll blame and I'll regret, as I reach old age
And you'll come to realize I did something foolish
That you'll pound me with questions, asking me "why?"
This is my nightmare
And here my heart pounds
I'm searching for the answer, I want to give you one

It's true that I ripped you away from your peace
It's true that I hauled you into a foreign land
It's true that I looked for good, true that I thought I'd find it
So that you'd benefit
I never faltered
Please don't indict me or rescind your faith

Please don't indict me, my children, understand me
Please don't strike me, I'm already at my grave
Please don't deride me or think ill of my name
As for the good for which I'm still searching
My children, it will be yours
And if I fail to provide it, my children, forgive me

I Won't Blunt My Knife

I won't deplete my strength hunting civets
Or waste my time; I know what's right
I won't blunt my knife on inedible meat

I won't blunt my knife on inedible meat
Angering God, and defiling myself
At the end of the fuss, there'll be nothing to show!

At the end of the fuss, there'll be nothing at all
Only self-inflicted bitterness, one's own unmaking
I respect my knife, it can't slaughter a cat

I respect my knife, I don't want it sullied
A civet is not my prey, as a hunter I know this
I'll leave it to the others who hunt inedible beasts!

Attacking the Jinni

The task I was given was to go find the jinni
To seize him securely and lock him up tight
I should close him in the bottle so he couldn't come free
Then go to his cave and quietly place it there

I was given all the tools and reliable materials
Cups were unwrapped for filling and for drinking
Sacrifices were made, talismans donned
And I traveled to where he was, with the intention to capture

I found there a huge jinni, no other could compare
From one end to the other, I couldn't possibly measure
In the middle of the forest, he sat on his throne
I didn't tremble, instead I was sure

I uttered some oaths, in voice enough to startle him
I told him, "Come here now, and fall to your knees,
Don't utter any *nyoo*, don't open your mouth!"
And he didn't refuse, he heeded my words

He knelt down on his knees, and lowered his face
In a very sweet tone, with a very soft voice
He told me: "Don't twist the lid tight, let me do your bidding!"
With pity, I teared up and thought, "Well, perhaps . . ."

I became his companion and realized he'd entrapped me
Like friends, we grew close over the years
Whatever I had against him, it all disappeared
And him to me the same, I became his companion

Back at our place they awaited my answer
That I should return and be given my reward
The hours turned to days, they never heard from me
The one I was sent to capture had become my friend

Where Are You, Joy?

I know you, joy, you are not one to stay
You are not one who settles in and forever remains
One moment you arrive and the next you've disappeared
But please do return

The shocking thing about humans: They fight over you
So you'll be with them forever, theirs alone and true
And even when you abandon them, you leave them with grief
They cry only for you

Even I yearn for the day you'll come back
Be mine in my heart, and spread through my limbs
If you had faith, joy, you would hear me singing
I pray that you'll come

Come to me, joy—I am calling for you to come
If only I can get you, I could find worth in the world
No more nights of regret, no more crying till I wake
Joy o joy

Some Things You Shouldn't Ask

Some things you shouldn't ask; the answers, you can't handle
They'll come to make you cry, they'll cause you to fall ill
Better to keep them quiet, they shouldn't give you trouble
If no answer will soothe you, it's better not to ask

It's better to keep quiet, avoid that difficult labor
You'll injure your heart; don't give it sorrow to carry
Look for answers yourself so you don't illicit rage
If no answer will soothe you, it's better not to ask

Look to answer for yourself, be the kind that doesn't ask
Satisfy yourself, don't look to others as your route
Be careful they don't wound you, with answers filled with rage
If no answer will soothe you, it's better not to ask

Judgment of Man

The judgment of man for his fellow man
In the gut is like poison, in the mind like a stone
Inflexible as iron, but a tempest when it blows
Even chilled it doesn't cool, its heat tends to grow

Its heat tends to grow, human against human
And its steam also lasts, trapped in the heart
Humidity building till the blood feels like fire
And even when it subsides, the wound does not heal

The wound does not heal, raw and open forever
Even if a person goes forward and never looks back
Judgment still surrounds him, above him and in front
And the sharp words of others break across his head

They break across his head, the words of his fellow man
Borrowing his happiness but never paying it back
In the end they draw out tears, which fall and then pool
Sleep then deserts him, not a wink to be found

Not a wink to be found, no sleep is on offer
Even when his eyes close, he hears only those words
They follow him everywhere, in a voice of fierce judgment
What's left leave to Him; Allah is your God.

If Things Go Bad

The day it goes bad and things veer off course
Everything you touch refuses to budge
Everything you say, even good, comes out wrong
You are left head in hands, collapsed in the dirt

The day you get angry, the world gives you fever
Knowledge abandons you, no matter how wise
Your judgment goes blank, and your intellect withers
You have nothing to add that doesn't bring doubt

That's a day for getting caught, for a person to get trapped
No matter how you refuse them, they always grind you down
You dare not raise your head nor lift your body upright
What remains is heaving breath and a heart that thumps with fear

Your heart thumps with fear, from its root to its stem
And your soul flies away, your very breath dissolves
Everything folds in, and the world itself changes
Only then can you see that there's truly no way out

I'm Afraid of Becoming Lost

I'm afraid of becoming lost and of losing my own children
I'm afraid of disappearing, being devoured by the world
Of my children leaving me, becoming no longer mine
Here in this place I have put myself

This place where I have put myself, and where I brought my children
I am afraid it will seize me, that they'll lock me up in cuffs
That I'll be unable to keep myself busy, that I'll begin defying God
That I become a person lost

I'm afraid of becoming lost, that tomorrow I won't find my portion
When I come before the Lord, and my book is handed to me
That I'll be faced with its pages, my own and those of my children
That that will be my undoing

I'm afraid of coming undone, when my days reach their end
That I won't be able to stand, that I won't have anyone of my own
That all will disclaim me, from my liver to my spleen
It's then that I want to leave

It's then that I want to leave, go back to my place
The place where if I collapse, I won't be left alone
Where there are handstaffs to lean on and people who are mine
Here I fear I'm lost!

The Ones Who Search for You

The relatives who search for you, I will tell them when I see them
I'll give them your news, and tell them you're still here
I'll let them know their prayers reach you even where you are
Wherever you go, brother, you go with their love

And the one who searches you out, with spite and resentment
He should stop with his disgrace, let him not chase shadows,
He should know you have what's yours, this onerous soul
I'll let him know how it is, may he faint from the shock

The ones standing in front of you, they are blocking you from seeing
You might hear with your ears, but your eyes cannot see
My advice, friend: Quit the back and move yourself to the center
Sit up front and keep watch, let those who'd block you fail

Those who want it search, and they'd take it if they could
but the ones who have it now, they keep it safe where they are
since the coconuts were tiny buds, they never leave it alone
they'll see it where it is, they cannot take it away

Ballot

I went out in early morning, arranged myself in line
I waited without tiring until the sun shone on my head
Until I reached the very front and the clerk looked up and asked:
"What is your name?" and I said it out loud

I pronounced my name, "So-in-so bin so-in-so."
And the sheha jumped. "What house is it you stay in?"
In fact, this sheha—he was also my neighbor
I told him, "Matuleni, and I'm sure you know the way"

So the sheha rose to his feet, looked inside his book
Among the listed names, he said, he didn't find me
"I don't know this man," he announced to the gathered crowd
All those years as neighbors, in an instant he denied me

Bitterness seized me, with sorrow and grief
I refused to leave, sat my body down and shouted
"Stop trammeling my rights!"
I was called over then and forcibly grabbed

The police arrested me with kicks and with punches
Laid me flat with clubs and threw me in the car
My blood was still flowing when they hid me in a cave
I stayed there for months, the election completed

Even when I was released, there was no compensation
I left the country instead and went to live abroad
And lo and behold, after a year, in my mailbox
I opened the notice, "You can vote if you want!"

This was a wonder to me, an unparalleled thing
This country that I'd come to as an absolute stranger
Today wanted my vote to be counted at their polls
The very right I'd had snatched from my hands in my home

I crumpled to the floor and wept without stopping
I remembered our homestead, my shehe, and that crowd
The suffering I endured to the point of imprisonment
Today in this foreign place, I'm told simply, "Here you go"

The Bones of the Migrants

The water has receded, the shore but wet lumps of sand,
Shards of bone out in the open now,
We see them,
What's left of bodies tossed in the current
When their boat went under
The dense, mature bones of men and women
And the slender ones of children
A community drowned
In the Mediterranean Sea,
As they fled calamity
Torture in Africa
Killings in the Arab world
Certain death in Asia
Others seeking sustenance, the promise of comfort in Europe

What disappeared into the ocean the ancestors have already named
It will make its way ashore, plain for all to see
Look at them
Look at the bones of the migrants
Spread along the shores of Europe
They didn't bury themselves or remain in the depths
But came to read us a message
Testimony of the migrants
The ones who fled their homes
Escaped disaster
Believing they would see
A day of grace
For themselves, for their children, at last

There, where the massive waves swallowed their voices
There, where the fierce winds toppled their boats
There, where the blackness of the sea engulfed them, mothers with their children
There, at the furthest reach of brutality, the end of their journey
There, where we stop up our ears, so as not to hear their cries
Where we shut our eyes, so as not see their wretchedness
There, yes there
Where they refused to die
It is there
That their bones return, confronting us on the beaches of Europe

On the beaches of Europe, laid bare as the tide recedes
The bones rise
With courage and conviction, they swear an oath
And speak their names
Herein is Juma, herein Moza, herein Raya, herein Asha and Mjaja
A grandfather of sixty, a tender youth of twenty, a child of only one
Not numbers but names
Humans, not beasts
These are people whose souls left them
This is life cut short
Arrested breath
The bones of the migrants have debts they are owed
Who will pay them?

I Am a Leaf

I am only a leaf
A leaf that's fallen from its tree
Morning is not yet evening, I am young and still quite fresh
Before the north winds blasted, still deep in rainy season
I was tugged from my limb
Tossed in the wind
And dropped in a raging stream

I came down into the water, and the current swept me away
Dumped into the ocean where I was carried off by the waves
At their riotous pace, I've already traveled far
Far from home
To a foreign land
Called Germany
Where I'm unknown

And here where I'm unfamiliar
The leaf tells the story of its tree
People gather as I sing
The story of my home
Its branches and boughs
Its trunk and roots
Its name is Zanzibar

While the Clay Is Wet

A wise cook
Never bends a fish
Once it's already dry
When it's fresh, she'll contort it
Season
Fry
And arrange
On the plate to be eaten

A skilled potter
Molds the clay
Only while it is wet
So that pots and stoves
Can be sculpted
When it's dry
The clay cracks
And can no longer be plied

A smart parent
Never curses the midwife
When she's in her birthing years
She'll praise her and
Treat her sweetly
So she still has an aid
For delivery
When the next belly comes

A traveler
Doesn't bad-mouth the sea
While still aboard the vessel
He waits for the anchor to settle
Complains
Only when he's sure
He's safe
on dry ground

Building a House from Afar

Building from afar requires heart
And steady patience
It requires you to be a man, with your purpose intact
Believe in God as your pillar, your spirit tenacious—
A rope that never breaks
Without these you'll never build

You'll never build a structure
Without holding on to your intention
You'll pack clay onto beams just to topple your walls
The scoffers will come and mock your exertion
In the end it might fail
It's happened plenty of times

We both know there are plenty—
Men who failed to advance
Who tried from afar to build their own homes
Despite all their effort, we watched them collapse
They gave up in defeat
Not for lack of means!

Those who failed to build
Weren't thwarted by funding
They had plenty for windows and louvers and rungs
But there are mishaps in building
If you aren't there to thatch
A home isn't simply soil and stones!

The making of a home is more than mud and stones
If you want to have ceilings and rooms and a door
And a roof over your head
Sometimes it just crumbles
If you're not there to oversee the work
It's trouble to build from afar!

You Are the Ones Who Love Me

You are the ones who love me: a rightful, even love
With the affection you give, indifferent to reward
With the hand you hold out, showing me the way
It is you and no one else

You are the ones who regard me, without the eye of "if"
Those who don't know try to shut me down
"If this's how it is . . ." "Things will never change"
Those are the limits they set

You are the ones who think of me, wherever in the world you are
The blessings you pray as darkness falls
You are the shields that keep me safe
In this you never tire

You are the ones who will want me, however it is I end up
Others see me as lacking, in rank and reputation
But to you I have these, and other things besides
You love me with all your heart

You are the ones who wait for me, even as the years pass by
No matter how long, without you I feel lost
At the end of it all, I can only come back
Who can withstand all this?

It is you who open your hearts and prompt others to unfold
You give me what I need, without a shred of spite
From the day I was born, it has been the same
You see me however I am

It is you who take on these burdens, who busy yourselves
With motherly tasks of birth and care
A mother's love is unique in the world
You are the ones who love me

Your Body Is War
Mahtem Shiferraw
Foreword by Kwame Dawes

In a Language That You Know
Len Verwey

Loving the Dying
Len Verwey

When We Only Have the Earth
Abdourahman A. Waberi
Translated by Nancy
Naomi Carlson

Logotherapy
Mukoma Wa Ngugi

*Breaking the Silence: Anthology
of Liberian Poetry*
Edited by Patricia Jabbeh Wesley

*Patricia Jabbeh Wesley:
Collected Poems, 1998–2020*
Patricia Jabbeh Wesley
Edited by Kwame Dawes
Marguerite L. Harrold,
Associate Editor
Introduction by Gabeba Baderoon

When the Wanderers Come Home
Patricia Jabbeh Wesley

*Seven New Generation African
Poets: A Chapbook Box Set*
Edited by Kwame Dawes
and Chris Abani
(Slapering Hol)

*Eight New-Generation African
Poets: A Chapbook Box Set*
Edited by Kwame Dawes
and Chris Abani
(Akashic Books)

*New-Generation African Poets:
A Chapbook Box Set (Tatu)*
Edited by Kwame Dawes
and Chris Abani
(Akashic Books)

*New-Generation African Poets:
A Chapbook Box Set (Nne)*
Edited by Kwame Dawes
and Chris Abani
(Akashic Books)

*New-Generation African Poets:
A Chapbook Box Set (Tano)*
Edited by Kwame Dawes
and Chris Abani
(Akashic Books)

*New-Generation African Poets:
A Chapbook Box Set (Sita)*
Edited by Kwame Dawes
and Chris Abani
(Akashic Books)

New-Generation African Poets:
A Chapbook Box Set (Saba)
Edited by Kwame Dawes
and Chris Abani
(Akashic Books)

New-Generation African Poets:
A Chapbook Box Set (Nane)
Edited by Kwame Dawes
and Chris Abani
(Akashic Books)

To order or obtain more information on these or other University of
Nebraska Press titles, visit nebraskapress.unl.edu. For more information
about the African Poetry Book Series, visit africanpoetrybf.brown.edu.

www.ingramcontent.com/pod-product-compliance
Lightning Source LLC
Chambersburg PA
CBHW021340090426
42742CB00008B/666